My Animal
Art Class

Nellie Shepherd

DK Publishing, Inc.

LONDON, NEW YORK, TORONTO, MELBOURNE,
MUNICH, AND DELHI

Editor Penny Smith
Designers Melanie Whittington, Jane Horne,
Wendy Bartlet, Lynne Moulding, Victoria Long
Managing Art Editor Diane Thistlethwaite
Production Rochelle Talary
Photography Stephen Hepworth
U.S. Editor Elizabeth Hester

For Anne Lumb (My Wonderful Aunt!)

ACKNOWLEDGMENTS
With thanks to: Alex, Alfie, Benjamin, Grace, Haydon, Heather, Helena, Jacob, Jessami, Jessica,
Lauren, Lucy, Max, Melissa, Mikey, Rebecca, Richard, Sam, Sophie, Tom, and Uzair for taking
part in the photographs; Jean Gollner, Anne Lumb, Wendy Morrison, James Pendrich,
Emma Hardy, Melena and Megan Smart (MMKS Logistics), David Hansel
(Memery Crystal), Peggy Atherton, Donna Huddleston, and Gwen Turner.

First published in the United States in 2003
by DK Publishing, Inc.
375 Hudson Street
New York, New York 10014
03 04 05 06 07 10 9 8 7 6 5 4 3 2 1

A catalog record
for this book is available
from the Library of Congress.

ISBN: 0-7894-9578-3

Color reproduction by GRB Editrice, Italy
Printed and bound in Italy by L.E.G.O.

Discover more at
www.dk.com

Where to find things

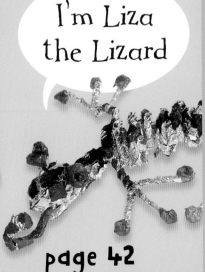

My Animal Art Class

This book is full of
animal characters
for you and
your children to
create together.

Making animals is so exciting!
In my art class, they can
look even more fantastic
than in real life! Flamingos
have glittery high heels,
hippos wear cool shades,
and monkeys are pink,
blue, and green! I hope
all the animals become
your friends and you have
a wild time making them!
Go for it!

Nellie Shepherd

Read Nellie's
tips on page 46
and be inspired!

Basic Materials

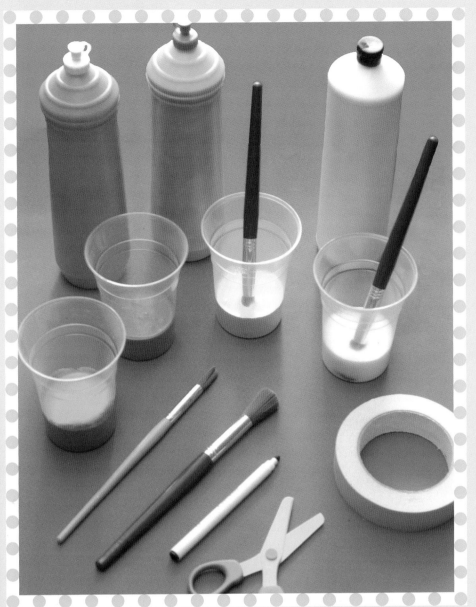

As well as the equipment pictured with each project, you will need the following basic materials:

poster board

construction paper

paint

felt-tip pens

glue

scissors

stapler

tape (masking tape is best)

cups (for paint and glue)

paintbrushes

pipe cleaners

play dough

straws

fabric

Keep your art kit in a box so you can find it easily!

Helping hand

All the projects in this book are designed for young children to make, but they should only be attempted under adult supervision. Extra care should be taken when using sharp equipment, such as scissors, staplers, and pipe cleaners, and with small objects that may cause choking. Only use non-toxic, water-soluble glue.

Bingo Flamingo

paper plate

pink fabric

glittery shoes

straws

Making Bingo Flamingo
Is as easy as pie.
You can take her for walks
And she might even fly!

Fab shoes!

6

You can use...

fabric

glitter

glue

poster board

straws

tissue paper

glitter

paper plate

Tot Tip! We made Bingo using pink fluffy fur fabric, but tissue paper works just as well.

How to make it!

cut

Cut Bingo's shoes, head, and neck out of poster board. Stick scrunched-up tissue paper on the poster board and all over Bingo's paper-plate body.

tape

Tape Bingo's neck to the back of her body. Tape her straw legs in place and tape her shoes to the ends of her legs.

bunch

For each wing, simply bunch together fabric or tissue paper. Tape the wings in place on Bingo's body.

stick

Stick on poster board circles for Bingo's eyes. Don't forget to glitter her heels. Now Bingo's ready to play!

Nice eyes!

8

Kid's talk
"I made my
Blingo with
stickerty stick
fluffy pieces."
Helena, age 3 ½

Zoe the Zebra

clothespin

spoon

plastic cup

I'm a Zebra called Zoe.
My stripes are just great.
If my legs start to wobble
Please stand me up straight!

You can use...

paint

plastic spoons

glue

clothespins

construction paper

tissue paper

plastic cups

Tot Tip! Use plenty of tape to hold Zoe together. She will wobble, but by clipping a clothespin to her tail you can make her balance.

Here We go!

tape

Cut the rim off one of the plastic cups and push it inside another to make Zoe's body. Tape it in place. You can start to decorate the cups any time you like.

push

Cut four holes in Zoe's body, then push a plastic spoon through each hole to make her legs. Push her legs into another cup to make her stand up.

cut

Take another cup and cut out a mouth and eyes (or paint them on later). Cut two ear holes and push two spoons into each. Clip together the spoon handles to make Zoe's neck.

Well done!

decorate

Make a hole in the top of Zoe's body and push her neck into it. Tape on a spoon tail and clip on a clothespin to make her balance. Decorate Zoe with paper, or paint mixed with glue.

Did you know?
When zebras are in a herd, their stripes make it hard to see where one zebra ends and another begins!

Gerry the Giraffe

Hi there! I'm Gerry
And I'm a giraffe.
My neck is so long,
It will make you laugh!

cotton swab

chomp
chomp
chomp

pencil

cardboard tube

14

You can use...

cork

cotton swab

tissue paper

cardboard tube

felt-tip pen

Pencils

rubber glove

Tot Tip! To make funky hooves, snip four fingertips off an old rubber glove. Make a hole in each and put them on Gerry.

15

How to make it!

bend

Bend a cardboard tube to form Gerry's head, neck, and body, or cut part-way throught a tube and hold it in place with tape. Push in pencils for Gerry's legs.

pull

Add Gerry's hooves by pulling the rubber-glove fingertips over the ends of his legs.

I can see you!

push

Make holes in Gerry's head and neck for his eyes, horns, and mane, and push in halved cotton swabs. Tape on poster-board ears and add a cotton swab for Gerry's tail.

paint

Mix a little glue with paint. Then paint Gerry and stick on tissue paper. Stick the cork in place for his nose. Draw on his mouth and eyes with felt-tip pen.

16

Did you know? Giraffes are the tallest animals on Earth!

Tilly the Turtle

paper bowl

flat scourer

I'm Tilly the Turtle.
I swim in the sea.
Make me from sponges.
Then have fun with me!

buttons

Hi!

18

You can use...

Tot Tip!

paint

flat scourers

beads

glue

yarn

buttons

paper bowl

sponges

Instead of beads and buttons, you can use dried beans or peas for Tilly's eyes and feet. Simply stick them in place with glue.

Bye!

19

You can do it!

paint

Tilly's the perfect pet! To make her, cut slits in a paper bowl for her head, tail, and legs. Then paint the bowl.

cut

Cut whatever shapes you like from flat scourers or sponges. Stick them on Tilly's back for decoration.

push

Cut out Tilly's head, tail, and legs from flat scourers or sponges. Then push them well into the slits in the bowl.

tape

Glue on buttons and beads for Tilly's eyes and feet. Finally, tape on a long piece of yarn and take Tilly for a walk!

Did you know?
Turtles scratch out nests in the ground. Some turtles lay as many as 200 eggs in one nest!

Whose pet are you?

Toothy Shark and Mr. Croc

My name is Toothy, and I am a shark.
I live in the sea, where it's deep and it's dark.
My friend Mr. Croc likes to join me for lunch.
We open up wide, then we munch, munch, munch!

Snip! Snap!

wooden spoon

Keep away— we bite!

Crunch! Crunch!

wooden fork

You can use...

paint

glue

sand

buttons

wooden fork

wooden spoon

poster board

Here we go!

Yum! Yum!

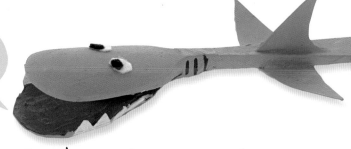

draw

For Toothy or Mr. Croc's jaw, draw around a spoon or fork on poster board. Cut it out and tape in place.

cut

Cut out fins, teeth, and a tail for Toothy, or spikes, legs, and a tail for Mr. Croc. Stick them in place.

paint

Now paint your animal however you want! If you want to stick things on Toothy or Mr. Croc, use paint mixed with a little glue.

sprinkle

We sprinkled our Mr. Croc with gre sand. Then we glued buttons onto folded poster board to make his eye We made Toothy's eyes from felt.

play

Let Toothy and Mr. Croc play together. Snap! Snip! Snap!

Caterpillar Jo

This creepy-crawly creature
Is colorful and bendy.
She's called Caterpillar Jo
And she's very, very friendly.

Let's play!

pot scourers

straw

26

You can use...

pot scourers

pipe cleaners

flat scourers

straws

You can do it!

push

Push pipe cleaners through both sides of a stack of pot scourers to make part of Jo's body. Make two or three sections of body this way.

join

Join the sections of Jo's body by twisting together the ends of the pipe cleaners.

bend

For the legs, attach pipe cleaners along both sides of Jo's body. Thread shortened straws onto the pipe cleaners. Bend the pipe cleaners to make Jo's feet.

tie together

Use a pipe cleaner to tie together two pot scourers for Jo's head. Push in twisted pipe-cleaner antennae.

cut

Cut out eyes from flat scourers. Push pipe cleaners through the eyes to attach them to Jo's head, and to make eyelashes.

Nice work!

28

Kid's talk
"They won't hurt you. They're only little creatures. They just creep around."
Mikey, age 3

Horace the Hippo

felt

poster board

pipe cleaners

Here's a very easy task:
Make this Horace Hippo mask.
Wear it when you want to play
And have a hippy, happy day!

You can use...

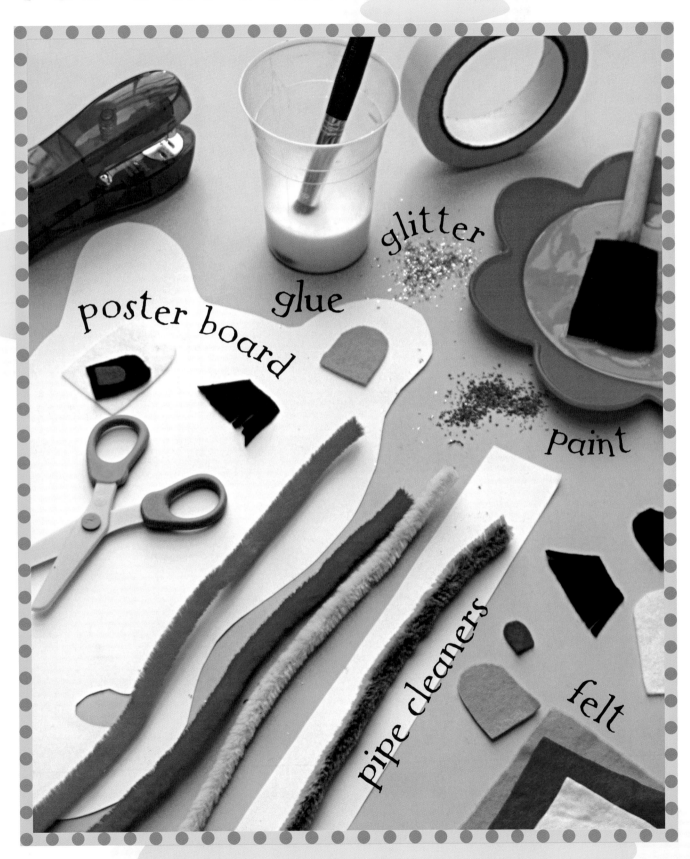

poster board

glue

glitter

paint

pipe cleaners

felt

How to make it!

draw

Draw a large hippo face on poster board and cut it out. To make a rounded, 3-D mask, cut slits in the ears and cheeks (as shown in this picture). Overlap the slits and tape or staple them in place.

staple

For the headband, staple together a strip of poster board to fit around your head. Staple two more strips to the band to go over the top of your head. Staple your mask to the band.

stick

Paint your mask, then stick on felt eyes and ears, and pipe-cleaner glasses. Add glitter, if you want.

Did you know?
A hippopotamus spends most of its day in water. Young hippos swim before they can walk!

Mane Man

I am king of the jungle
And fierce you will agree.
I roar really loud
And I am very proud.
No one will argue with me!

You can use...

glue

felt

Paint

tissue paper

glitter

yarn

poster board

Tot Tip!

Hold the mask over your face and mark the eyes in the right place before you cut them out.

How to make it!

draw

Draw a lion-shaped face on poster board and cut it out. Paint the face if you like. Cut a nose and mouth out of felt and stick them in place. Stick felt or poster-board triangles around the face for a mane. Add felt whiskers, too.

rip

Cut out a long strip of poster board to make the back of the mane. Rip tissue paper into strips, then glue them on the mane. The more tissue paper you use, the wilder your mane will be!

Be careful here.

roar!

Staple the mane onto your lion mask. Add glitter to your mask if you want. Tape on a piece of yarn to secure the mask to your head. Then put it on and roar like a lion!

Did you know?
Only the male lion
has a mane. He lives
in a family group
called a pride.

Monkey Madness

poster board

I'm hooked!

We're a group of funny monkeys
And we swing high in the trees.
We get up to lots of trouble
And hope that no one sees!

You can use...

poster board

glue

buttons

ponytail holders

string

fabric

You can do it!

Copy me!

copy

Try copying this monkey shape on poster board. You need one big mama monkey and lots of small baby monkeys. Now cut them out.

cut

Cut out poster board shapes for the monkeys' faces, ears, and tummies and glue them in place. Stick on buttons or poster board for eyes, noses, and mouths, or simply draw them on.

stick

Make clothes for the mama by sticking on fabric leaves and string bows. Thread ponytail holders onto string for a necklace, and make earrings from ponytail holders or whatever you choose.

link

All the baby monkeys hang from the mama and each other. How many ways can you link them?

40

Did you know?
Most real monkeys have tails. Some monkeys can hang from their tails, keeping their hands free to reach tasty fruit!

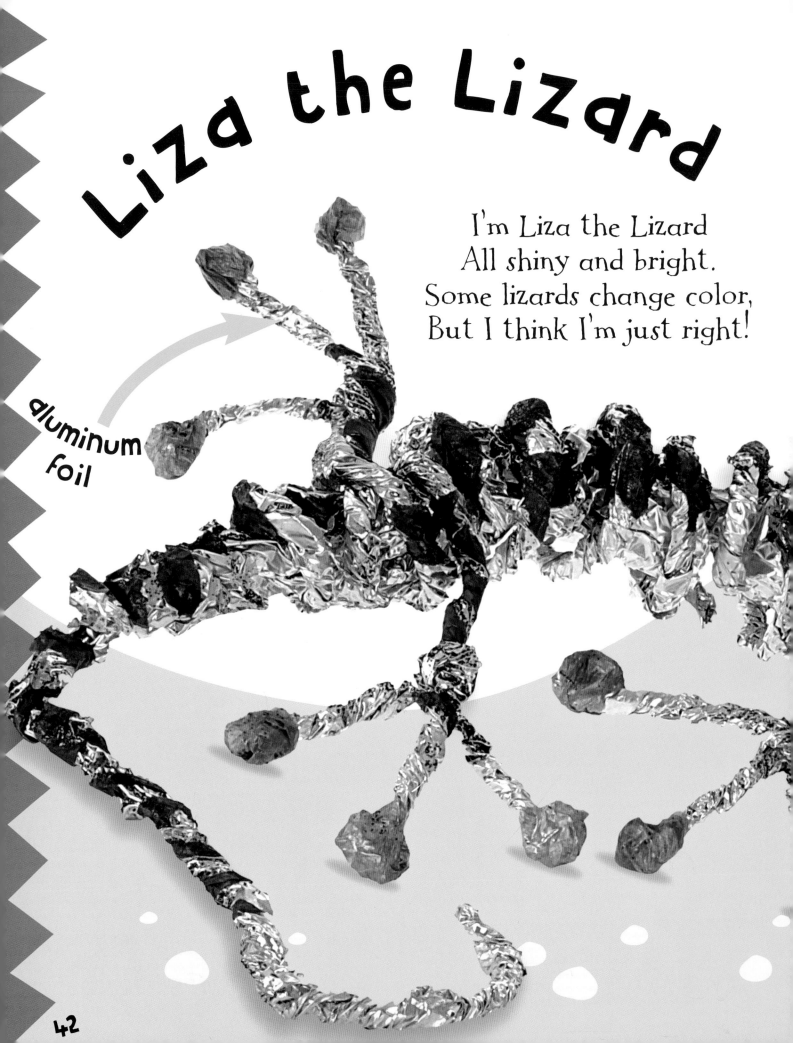

Liza the Lizard

I'm Liza the Lizard
All shiny and bright.
Some lizards change color,
But I think I'm just right!

aluminum foil

42

You can use...

glue

aluminum foil

tissue paper

tissue paper

I'm soooo shiny!

How to make it!

I'm scrunched up!

scrunch

Take a long strip of aluminum foil and scrunch one end to make Liza's head. Scrunch the rest of the piece into a long lizard-like body that gets thinner toward the end of the tail.

twist

For Liza's legs, twist two more pieces of foil and wind them around her body. Add smaller twists of foil for her toes.

wrap

Twist more small strips of aluminum foil to make Liza's curly tongue and sticking-up eyes. Wrap them around her head or glue them on.

I'm in a twist!

glue

To give Liza color, glue pieces of tissue paper onto her. No two Lizas are the same. What color is yours?

Did you know?
The chameleon
lizard can change
the color of
its skin!

Nellie's Knowledge

I've been teaching my art class to children for over ten years. Along the way, I've discovered a few tips that make the classes a lot of fun—and help bring out the creativity in all of us!

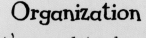

Organization

It's good to have all the things you need before you start. But if you don't have something, just improvise and use something else!

Inspiration

Look at all sorts of odds and ends. What can you make them into? Challenge yourself and be inspired!

Fun factor!

Think about inviting friends over to join in. Play music and have a story break. It makes such a difference.

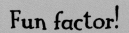

Making a mess

Art is a messy business! Just put down lots of newspaper, relax, and create. It's worth it!

Encouragement

Encouragement is great for building confidence and creativity: one hundred percent encouragement equals one hundred percent creativity!

Positive attitude

We're positive! In my art classes we never say we can't do something, because we simply can!

Making choices

Children's concentration is greatest when they choose the things they want to make. They make their own decisions from the start and they see them through.

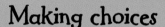

Displaying

Displaying as well as talking about children's art shows it's important. Go for it, put it up on the wall!

We've had lots of fun. Good-bye